Insect World
Mosquitoes

by Mari Schuh

Bullfrog Books

Ideas for Parents and Teachers

Bullfrog Books let children practice reading informational text at the earliest reading levels. Repetition, familiar words, and photo labels support early readers.

Before Reading

• Discuss the cover photo. What does it tell them?

• Look at the picture glossary together. Read and discuss the words.

Read the Book

• "Walk" through the book and look at the photos. Let the child ask questions. Point out the photo labels.

• Read the book to the child, or have him or her read independently.

After Reading

• Prompt the child to think more. Ask: Have you ever seen a mosquito? Did it buzz? Did it bite?

Bullfrog Books are published by Jump!
5357 Penn Avenue South
Minneapolis, MN 55419
www.jumplibrary.com

Library of Congress Cataloging-in-Publication Data

Schuh, Mari C., 1975- author.
 Mosquitoes / by Mari Schuh.
    pages cm. -- (Insect world)
 Summary: "This photo-illustrated book for early readers tells how mosquitoes find food and briefly describes their life cycle. Includes picture glossary"-- Provided by publisher.
 Audience: Ages 5 to 8.
 Audience: K to grade 3.
 Includes bibliographical references and index.
 ISBN 978-1-62031-085-4 (hardcover) --
ISBN 978-1-62496-153-3 (ebook)
 1. Mosquitoes--Juvenile literature. I. Title.
II. Series: Schuh, Mari C., 1975- Insect world.
 QL536.S38 2015
 595.77'2--dc23
                                   2013039887

Series Editor: Rebecca Glaser
Series Designer: Ellen Huber
Book Designer: Anna Peterson
Photo Researcher: Kurtis Kinneman

All photos by Shutterstock except: Alex Wild, 12–13; Biosphoto, 23br; iStock, 1, 13 (inset), 18, 23bl; Jinfeng Zhang|Dreamstime.com, 6; TurnipTowers/SuperStock, 16–17

Printed in the United States of America at Corporate Graphics, in North Mankato, Minnesota.
6-2014
10 9 8 7 6 5 4 3 2 1

Dedicated to St. John Vianney School in Fairmont, MN—MS

Table of Contents

Buzzing Bugs

Buzz! Buzz!

What is that noise?

A mosquito.

Buzz! Buzz!
It hears.
It smells.

male
mosquito

6

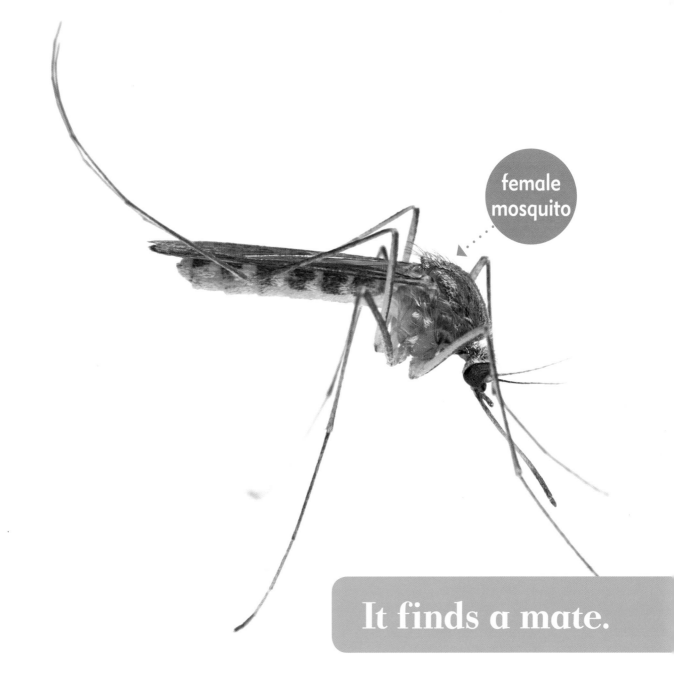

female
mosquito

It finds a mate.

They look for food.

Here is a flower.

The male drinks
the nectar.

The female likes
nectar, too.

But she will need blood.

Why?

It helps her eggs grow.

drinking
tube

She sees Emma.

She lands.

See her long drinking tube?

She pokes it into
Emma's skin.

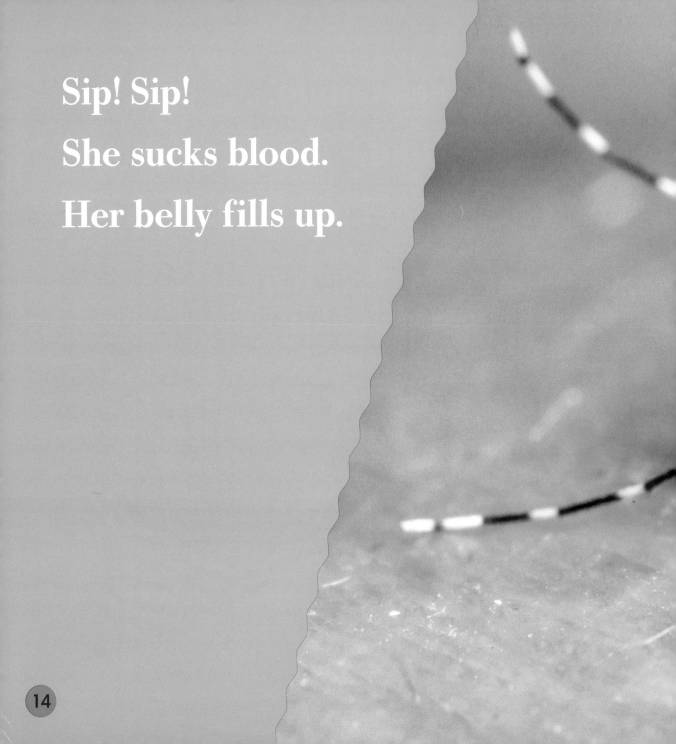

Sip! Sip!
She sucks blood.
Her belly fills up.

14

blood

She flies away.

It is time to lay eggs.

She looks for water.
Then she lays eggs.

eggs

18

There are more than 100!

The eggs grow and grow.
Now they are mosquitoes.
Buzz! Buzz!

Parts of a Mosquito

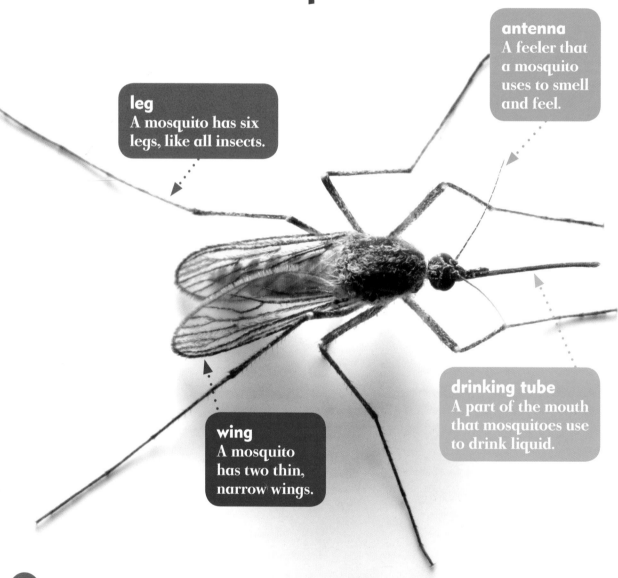

antenna
A feeler that a mosquito uses to smell and feel.

leg
A mosquito has six legs, like all insects.

drinking tube
A part of the mouth that mosquitoes use to drink liquid.

wing
A mosquito has two thin, narrow wings.

Picture Glossary

blood
A red liquid found inside the bodies of animals.

male
An animal that can father young.

female
An animal that can lay eggs or give birth to young.

mate
A male or female partner of a pair of animals.

Index

To Learn More

Learning more is as easy as 1, 2, 3.

1) Go to www.factsurfer.com

2) Enter "mosquitoes" into the search box.

3) Click the "Surf" button to see a list of websites.

With factsurfer.com, finding more information is just a click away.